MW00886525

BEST SWING TRA
GUIDE

A Complete Guide on Technical Indicators for Swing Trading

FRANKLIN FOSTER

Table of Contents

Technical Indicators...................................... 6

Technical Indicator: What It Is 6

Functions and What You Get From Technical Indicators 7

Proper Use of Technical Indicators.................... 8

Example of Technical Indicators...................... 11

Technical Analysis Indicators 15

1. Moving Averages 16

2. RSI – Relative Strength Index 18

3. Volume... 19

4. Bollinger Bands Indicator 20

5. Accumulation and Distribution Line 21

6. The Average Directional Index, ADX...........23

7. Aroon Technical Indicator........................... 24

Types of Technical Indicators.......................27

Popular Technical Indicators for Newbie Traders.. 30

Exponential Moving Averages (EMA): 50 and 200 Days... 30

Bollinger Bands 32

Relative Strength Index 34

Moving Average Convergence-Divergence (MACD).. 34

On-Balance Volume (OBV).............................. 38

On Choosing Technical Indicators 40

How to use each Technical Analysis (Indicators) for swing trading 41

Simple Moving Averages................................... 41

Looking for cross overs................................... 44

Exponential moving averages 46

Bollinger Bands... *50*

True Range and Average True Range 54

ADX and Moving Average Convergence/Divergence (MACD) 55

Choose your indicators 57

Moving Averages..*59*

Simple Moving Averages versus Exponential Moving Averages.. 60

How to Use Both Averages 61

Moving Averages: Advantages......................... 64

Moving Averages: Disadvantages 64

Testing Price Boundaries 65

Bottom Line 65

How to use indicators from the Moves of Big Players 67

Information Revealed by the RSI Index 68

Simple Ways of Trading the RSI Indicator 69

Trading an RSI in the Oversold Region 70

Trading an RSI Index in the Overbought Region 70

Selling or Trading on an RSI Index Divergence 71

Tips on How to Use the RSI Effectively 71

The Downside of the Relative Strength Indicator 73

Learn and Benefit From Moves of the Big Players 74

Support and Resistance 75

What Novices Do Not Know 76

Tips on Profiting from Support and Resistance 78

What Indicators Mean to You as a Beginner 79

Learn to Separate Substance from Fluff 82

Watch Fund Managers 83

Watch Major Stocks 83

Have your Own Set of Investing Rules............................... 84

What is mean reversion trading? 87

Summary of Technical Analysis – Indicator Tools **88**

Support and Resistance Levels **91**

Diagonal Lines..95

How to Use Support and Resistance Levels........................ 96

Moving Averages... **98**

Simple vs. Exponential Moving Averages 99

Moving Average Time Periods...104

The Golden Cross and the Death Cross...............................107

Moving Averages in Range-Bound Stocks and Markets .. 108

How to Use Moving Averages...109

Relative Strength Index **110**

How to Use the RSI Indicator... 112

MACD: Convergence and Divergence **113**

How to Use the MACD 118

Average True Range **119**

How to Use the ATR Indicator 121

Technical Indicators

Technical Indicator: What It Is

The OHLC (open, high, low, and close) price of a stock over a period of time forms the price data of that stock or security. Now when the price data of a particular security is passed through a set of mathematical functions or formulas, a sequence of data points are created. This is what is known as a technical indicator. So to give it a proper definition: a technical indicator is a series or sequence of data points that are generated through the application of mathematical formulas to the price data of a particular security. Several other indices such as the volume of a stock may also be included into the formula to generate the data points.

I am going to save you the headache of how the formula is applied to the price data and all the computations involved in coming up with a technical indicator. All you need to know as a beginner is that technical indicators are displayed graphically on top or below the chart of a security or stock. And it is there to aid you in your market analysis – to compare the stock's chart with the information on the technical indicator. The more in agreement they are, the better decision you can make.

Before you go hunting for the perfect technical indicator that will show you all the good trades, be aware that these indicators are not 100 percent accurate all of the time. They can signal a false buy or sell alert. So be warned.

Functions and What You Get From Technical Indicators

While the stock chart shows you price action, technical indicators show you other information about the same stock from a different vantage point.

Basically, the functions of technical indicators are summarized below:

For Confirmation: Throughout this guide, I have advised that you should not base your trading decisions solely on one tool. A technical indicator can serve as a tool that you use in confirming whatever you deduce from price actions on a chart. For example, when you observe that a stock has broken a support level, you could look at the OBV to confirm if there is a low reading to indicate that there is an actual weakness.

OBV means On Balance Volume; it is a technical indicator.

For Calling Attention: Technical indicators can draw the trader's attention to study price actions more carefully. It can prompt you to a variety of alerts that can really save you from some serious financial damage. For example, you may be prompted to look out for a break in support level when momentum is declining.

For Predicting Price Direction: A technical indicator can also serve as a tool for predicting what side future prices will lean towards – up or down.

Proper Use of Technical Indicators

No One Size Fits All: Different stocks may cause the same indicator to behave differently. In using technical indicators, it is important to know that different indicators tend to work well for different stocks. With continuous practice and application, you will come to discover which indicator will serve you best for your chosen stocks.

To Indicate: There is no single tool that has all the trading answers! Have I said that enough times yet?

That is because it is of vital importance to keep that in mind. In that sense, it is important to note that one proper way to use a technical indicator is to see them as tools that only point to the likelihood of an outcome.

They must be used in combination with price action. A technical indicator does not directly represent price action; what it does is to present you with information about its own generated or computed results from price data. There are times when a technical indicator will signal you to buy or sell, yet they could be very wrong. If you do not verify each signal with what the stock chart is telling you, it may lead to fatal trading mistakes.

The bottom line is this: technical indicators aid you but they do not do the trading for you. Ultimately, you are the one who decides what and when to trade based on signals from indicators and other analysis.

Use Time Tested Indicators: The proliferation of technical indicators seems to be on a constant rise. Some newer computer programs even provide users (traders) the choice of developing custom made indicators! But with all of the numerous new indicators available at our beck and call, it seems they do not offer anything too unique or new from others in existence before them. As a matter of fact, I would advise that as a beginner, you stick to time tested indicators to avoid being sent on a wild goose chase.

A Few Is Good Enough: As mentioned above, there are several technical indicators available today. But you really do not need all of them. Heck! You do not even need more than three good technical indicators to succeed in a proper analysis. What matters is that you are well acquainted with the few you use. The fewer the number of indicators, the better you will learn and know how to use them.

A Few Complementary Indicators: What would be the point of having three indicators that all function almost exactly the same way? That's a huge waste of time and resources. When you are picking out your few indicators, make sure that you select indicators that complement each other. That is to say, select indicators that perform functions that add to the functions of the other(s). If you decide to use only two indicators, for example, it doesn't make much sense to choose the Accumulation/Distribution Line and Chaikin Money Flow (CMF) as your only two technical indicators. Both of them perform the same function which is to show if money is coming in or going out of a stock by combining volume and price.

Example of Technical Indicators

There are very many technical indicators; however, I've listed below a few which you may find useful. You can research more to find the ones that best suit you. Generally, technical indicators are grouped into overlays and oscillators.

Overlays are technical indicators which are plotted on top of a chart above the stock price. They usually have the same scale as price. Examples include Pivot Points and Moving Averages.

On the other hand, oscillators are indicators that swing or fluctuate between set levels and are plotted below or above prices on a chart.

Accumulation/Distribution Line: This shows whether money is coming in or going out of a stock by combining volume and price.

Average Directional Index (ADX): This shows whether a particular stock is oscillating or trending.

Average True Range (ATR): This measures the volatility of a stock.

Bollinger Bands: This shows the lower and upper limits of price movements.

Change Trend Meter (CTM): This measures the trend of a stock and scores the trend's strength using several indicators over a period of six-time frames.

Chandelier Exit: This can be used in setting up trailing stop-loss for all positions.

Commodity Channel Index (CCI): Shows variation from the usual price of a stock.

Correlation Coefficient: Shows the level of relationship between two stocks or securities within a specific period.

Decision Point Price Momentum Oscillator (PMO): This follows the rate of change of a stock closely.

Ichimoku Cloud: This defines resistance and support levels, provide trading signals, measures momentum, and show the direction of a stock's trend.

Moving Average Convergence/Divergence Oscillator (MACD): This is an oscillator that shows momentum based on the variation between two Exponential Moving Averages.

Moving Averages: These are overlays on a chart that display the average price of a stock over a given period.

On Balance Volume (OBV): This shows whether money is coming in or going out of a stock by combining volume and price in a simple way.

Pivot Points: This is an overlay on a chart which displays reversal points above prices in a downtrend and below prices in the case of an uptrend.

Relative Strength Index (RSI): Shows the strength of a stock's trend.

Stochastic Oscillator: Shows the performance of a stock's price in comparison with its past movement.

Volume by Price: This is an overlay on a chart which shows a horizontal histogram that displays the activities that occur at different price levels.

Vortex Indicator: Indicates the beginning of a new trend, and also defines a current trend.

Williams %R: This indicator draws on Stochastics to find out oversold and overbought levels.

Zig Zag: This is an overlay on a chart that displays filtered price movements which are above a specific percentage.

You have learned the following:

- Technical indicators only indicate. They are not 100% accurate at all times.
- Technical indicators are used for confirming, calling attention, and predicting future price direction.
- Not all technical indicators suit all stocks or securities.
- Limit your use of technical indicators to a few dependable ones.
- Let your choice of indicators complement each other.

Technical Analysis Indicators

Technical indicators refer to mathematical models that strive to predict a security or market's future price movements using data such as historical prices, trading volume, and open interest. Some of the most popular technical indicators traders use to time their trades include the moving averages (MA), moving average convergence divergence (MACD), relative strength indicator (RSI), Money Flow Index (MFI), Stochastics, and Bollinger Bands. Best Indicators for Swing Traders

There are plenty of indicators that traders and investors use to enhance their trades. We shall review just a few of these and discover the best way of applying them to our trades in order to maximize profitability. It is crucial to understand that none of these indicators will make you profitable from the onset. Therefore, do not stress over trying to find the best or most profitable trade indicators. Instead, focus more on learning about a couple of extremely effective indicators as well as the strategies and methods used alongside them. Experts believe that trading strategies are more profitable when you apply the few indicators that you have mastered.

1. Moving Averages

Moving averages are among the most important trade indicators used by swing traders. They are defined as lines drawn across a chart and are determined based on previous prices. Moving averages are really to understand, yet they are absolutely useful when it comes to trading the markets. They are extremely useful to all kinds of traders, including swing traders, day traders, intra-day traders, and long-term investors.

You need to ensure that you have a number of moving averages plotted across your trading charts all with different time periods. For instance, you can have the 100-day moving average, the 50-day, and the 9-day MA. This way, you will obtain a much broader overview of the market and be able to identify much stronger reversals and trends.

Once you have plotted and drawn the moving averages on your charts, you can then use them for a number of purposes. The first is to identify the strength of a trend. Basically, what you need to do is to observe the lines and gauge their distance from the current stock price.

A trend is considered weak if the trend and the current price are far from the relative MA. The farther they are then, the weaker the trend is. This makes it easier for traders to note any possible reversals and also identify exit and entry points. You should use Moving Averages together with additional indicators—for instance, the volume.

Moving averages can also be used to identify trend reversals. When you plot multiple moving averages, they are bound to cross. If they do, then this implies a couple of things. For instance, crossing MA lines indicate a trend reversal. If these cross after an uptrend, then it means that the trend is about to change direction and a bearish one is about to appear.

However, some trend reversals are never real, so you have to be careful before calling out one. Many traders are often caught off guard by these false reversals. Therefore, confirm them before trading using other tools and methods. Even then, the moving average is a very vital indicator. They enable traders to get a true feel and understanding of the markets.

2. RSI – Relative Strength Index

Another crucial indicator that is commonly used by swing traders and other traders is the RSI or relative strength index. This index is also an indicator that evaluates the strength of the price of a security that you may be interested in. The figure indicated is relative and provides traders with a picture of how the stock is performing relative to the markets. You will need information regarding volatility and past performance. All traders, regardless of their trading styles, need this useful indicator. Using this relative evaluation tool gives you a figure that lies between 1 and 100.

Tips on RSI Use

The relative strength index is ideally used for identifying divergence. Divergence is used by traders to note trend reversals. We can say that divergence is a disagreement or difference between two points. There are bearish and bullish divergent signals. Very large and fast movements in the markets sometimes produce false signals. This is why it advisable to always use indicators together with other tools.

You can also use the RSI to identify oversold and overbought conditions. It is crucial that you are able to identify these conditions as you trade because you will easily identify corrections and reversals. Sometimes, securities are overbought at the markets—when this situation occurs, it means that there is a possible trend reversal, and usually the emerging trend is bearish. This is often a market correction. Basically, when a security is oversold, it signals a correction or bullish trend reversal. However, when it's overbought, it introduces a bearish trend reversal.

The theory aspect of this condition requires a ratio of 70:30. This translates to 70% overvalued or over purchased and 30% undervalued or oversold. However, in some cases, you might be safer going with a ratio of 80:20 just to prevent false breakouts.

3. Volume

When trading, the volume is a crucial indicator and constitutes a major part of any trading strategy. As a trader, you want to always target stocks with high volumes as these are considered liquid. How many traders, especially new ones, often disregard volume and look at other indicators instead.

While volume is great for liquidity purposes, it is also desirable for trend. A good trend should be supported by volume. A large part of any stock's volume should constitute part of any trend for it to be a true and reliable trend.

Most of the time traders will observe a trend based on price action. You need to also be on the lookout for new money which means additional players and volume. If you note significant volumes contributing to a trend, then you can be confident about your analysis. Even when it comes to a downtrend, there should be sufficient volumes visible for it to be considered trustworthy. A lack of volume simply means a stock has either been undervalued or overvalued.

4. Bollinger Bands Indicator

One of the most important indicators that you will need is the Bollinger band indicator. It is a technical indicator that performs two crucial purposes. The first is to identify sections of the market that are overbought and oversold. The other purpose is to check the market's volatility.

This indicator consists of 3 distinct moving averages. There is a central one which is an SMA or simple moving average and then there two on each side of the SMA. These are also moving averages but are plotted on either side of the central SMA about 2 standard deviations away. These bands can be clearly viewed in the diagram below.

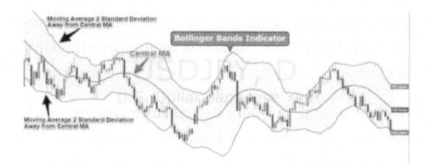

5. Accumulation and Distribution Line

Another indicator that is widely used by swing traders is the accumulation/distribution line. This indicator is generally used to track the money flow within a security. The money that flows into and out of a particular stock provides useful information for your analysis.

The accumulation/distribution indicator compares very well with another indicator, the OBV, or the on-balance volume indicator. The difference, in this case, is that it considers the trading range as well as the closing price of a stock. The OBV only considers the trading range for a given period.

When a security closes out close to its high, then the accumulation/distribution indicator will add weight to the stock value compared to closing out close to the mid-point. Depending on your needs and sometimes the calculations, you may also want to use the OBV indicator.

You can use this indicator to confirm an upward trend. For instance, when it is trending upwards, you will observe buying interest because the security will close at a point that is higher than the mid-range. However, when it closes at a point that is lower than the mid-range, then the volume is indicated as negative, and this indicates a declining trend.

While using this indicator, you will also want to be on the lookout for divergence. When the accumulation/distribution begins to decline while the price is going up, then you should be careful because this signals a possible reversal. On the other hand, if the trend starts to ascend while the price is falling, then this probably indicates a possible price rise in the near future. It is advisable to ensure that your internet and other connections are extremely fast, especially when using these indicators, as time is essential.

6. The Average Directional Index, ADX

Another tool or indicator that is widely used by swing traders is the average directional index, the ADX. This indicator is basically a trend indicator, and its purpose is largely to check the momentum and strength of a trend. A trend is believed to have directional strength if the ADX value is equal to or higher than 40. The directional could be upwards or downward based on the general price direction. However, when the ADX value is below 20, then we can say that there is no trend or there is one, but it is weak and unreliable.

You will notice the ADX line on your charts as it is the main line and is often black in color. There are other lines that can be shown additionally. These lines are DI- and DI+ and in most cases are green and red in color, respectively. You can use all the three lines to track both the momentum and the trend direction.

7. Aroon Technical Indicator

Another useful indicator that you can use is the Aroon indicator. This is a technical indicator designed to check if a particular financial security is trending. It also checks to find out whether the security's price is achieving new lows or new highs over a given period of time.

You can also use this technical indicator to discover the onset of a new trend. It features two distinct lines, which are the "Aroon down" line and the "Aroon up" line. A trend is noted when the "Aroon up" line traverses across the "Aroon down" line. To confirm the trend, then the "Aroon up" line will get to 100-point mark and stay there.

The reverse holds water as well. When the "Aroon down" line cuts below the "Aroon up" line, then we can presume a downward trend. To confirm this, we should note the line that is getting close to the 100-point mark and staying there.

This popular trading tool comes with a calculator which you can use to determine a few things. If the trend is bullish or bearish, then the calculator will let you know. The formulas used to determine this refer to the most recent highs and lows. When the Aroon values are high, then recent values were used; when they are low, the values used were less recent. Typical Aroon values vary between 0 and 100. Figures that are close to 0 indicate a weak trend while those closer to 100 indicate a strong trend.

The bullish and bearish Aroon indicators can be converted into one oscillator. This is done by making the bearish one range from 0 to -100 while the bullish one ranges from 100 to 0. The combined indicator will then oscillate between 100 and -100. 100 will indicate a strong trend, 0 means there is no trend while -100 implies a negative or downward trend.

This trading tool is pretty easy to use. What you need to is first obtain the necessary figures then plot these on the relevant chart. When you then plot these figures on the chart, watch out for the two key levels. These are 30 and 70. Anything above the 70-point mark means the trend is solid while anything below 30 implies a weak trend.

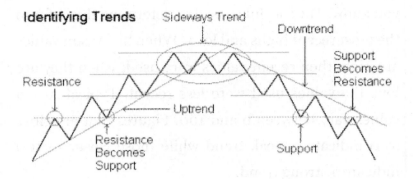

Identifying Trends

Sideways Trend

Downtrend

Support
Becomes
Resistance

Resistance

Resistance
Becomes
Support

Uptrend

Support

Types of Technical Indicators

Being a form of technical analysis, indicators focus on a security's historical trading data such as price, volume and open interest. There are two general types of technical indicators:

Oscillators: These indicators feature numbers that fluctuate between a specified minimum and maximum number, which are plotted below or above an existing price chart. The RSI, MACD and stochastic oscillator fall under this category.

These indicators are plotted on top of the actual prices on a security's price chart. MA and Bollinger Bands fall under this category.

Traders normally use multiple technical indicators when they time their trades. Given the myriad number of available technical indicators, traders need to choose and focus on a couple of indicators only and master them. The right indicators can result in trading riches while wrong ones can plunder any trader with huge trading losses. Because of their highly quantitative nature, they can be easily incorporated into any trading software or platform for easier use.

Many newbie traders make the mistake of choosing technical indicators based on what other, more seasoned traders use, even if they don't fully understand how such indicators work. Worse, many newbie traders try to use as many indicators as possible "just to make sure."

Don't make the same mistake when starting to use technical indicators for swing trading because this is one instance where the old saying "the more, the merrier" isn't applicable. The purpose of using technical analysis, which includes technical indicators, is to simplify the profitable trading process. Using too many technical indicators will make trading more complicated, especially when they give seemingly contradictory signals because they look at the market through different angles.

Trend indicators, which analyze the market or security's price trend, e.g., upward, downward or sideways; Mean reversion indicators, which measure a price swing's magnitude before it retracts or pulls back; and Volume indicators, which measure the number of buy-up (bullish) and sell-down (bearish) trades to estimate investors' general sentiment about a security.

On the other hand, leading indicators indicate a trend that's about to reverse or start. These indicators include:

Relative strength indicators, which measures buying and selling strength or pressure; Momentum indicators, which measures the speed of price changes over time to measure a trend's momentum; and Volume indicators.

Choosing and setting up technical indicators for profitable swing trading depends on a trader's trading style, which requires sufficient experience and skill. Given this, how can newbie swing traders choose the optimal technical indicators for them?

The best general approach is to start with using a couple of the most popular technical indicators first. There are reasons why they're the most popular, and one of them is many traders find them to be profitable trading tools. Over time, try to gauge whether they're working or if they need some tweaking.

Popular Technical Indicators for Newbie Traders

Exponential Moving Averages (EMA): 50 and 200 Days

Moving averages refer to the average prices of securities over a specific period of time, let's say the last 10 trading days. Because the average only considers the last X-number of trading days, the price population from which averages are computed change every day.

Let's say you're using a 10-day moving average. Let's say there are 22 trading days last month. On the 10th trading day, the ten-day average closing price is the average closing price from the first to the tenth trading day of last month. On the 11th trading day, the average closing price is that from the second to the eleventh trading day, and so on.

The reason it's called a moving average is because the population from which the average is computed moves or changes as time goes by. The last X number of days today will be different from that of tomorrow. This is called a simple moving average.

Exponential moving averages are different from simple ones in that the latest prices have more weight in computing the average compared to the oldest ones. The logic behind giving more premium to the most recent data is relevance; i.e., the market data becomes less relevant as time goes by.

How do traders use moving averages? They usually do it in pairs, a short-term moving average and a longer-term one. One of the most popular pairs traders use for exponential moving averages are the 50-day and the 200-day moving averages.

On an upward trending security, the short-term moving average will be above the long-term one by virtue of the latter using more prices from the past, which are lower. The moment that the short-term moving average crosses over and goes below the long-term moving average, it's a signal that the bullish trend has ended and a bearish one has already begun. This is a "sell" signal."

On a downward trending security, the short-term moving average will be lower than the long-term one. This is because longer moving averages trail shorter ones, which means it takes into consideration more prices from the past, which in this case are higher prices. The moment that short-term moving average cross above the long-term one for the period, it's a signal that the bearish trend has ended and a bullish one has begun already. This is a "buy" signal.

Bollinger Bands

Bollinger bands are technical indicators that use standard deviations to identify a band or price range in which a security's moving average is expected to oscillate or move. But how are Bollinger bands used in swing trading?

Traders who use this technical indicator believe that a security becomes more overbought when its price moves closer to the upper band and more oversold when it moves closer to the lower one. John Bollinger, the creator of this technical indicator, has 22 rules governing the trading use of his bands.

Another way traders use this indicator is through the "squeeze," i.e., the width of the band. Since the upper and lower bands represent upper and lower standard deviations of the price and it's a measure of volatility, the price of a security is deemed to become more volatile the wider the band becomes. The narrower it gets, the less volatile the price becomes.

With increased volatility comes the potential for greater price swings, which is what swing traders are looking for. Therefore, when the bands widen, it's a signal for swing traders to take positions because good swing trading opportunities are present. On the other hand, a narrowing band signals that it's time to close a position because less volatility means less meaningful price swings.

It's important to note the limitations of Bollinger bands to avoid using them erroneously. One of them is that Bollinger bands only indicate volatility and possible swing trading opportunities, not trend reversals. This leads us to the second limitation of Bollinger bands: they're not stand-alone trading systems. Even John Bollinger himself suggests that this indicator be used together with other indicators such as the relative strength index (RSI), moving averages, and on-balance volume.

Relative Strength Index

This is a technical indicator that measures a price movement's momentum through the size of recent price movements. It evaluates whether a particular security's price is already oversold or overbought.

The RSI's value ranges from 0 to 100 only, represented by a line graph that moves in between these two values. Traders interpret an RSI of above 70 as a security becoming overvalued already, i.e., overbought, which makes a trend reversal or price correction highly possible. An RSI of below 30 indicates that a security has become oversold or undervalued, which makes an upward reversal or correction in a downward trend highly likely.

Moving Average Convergence-Divergence (MACD)

MACD is a technical indicator that follows price trends by using two exponential moving averages (EMAs) for a security's price – the 12-period and 26-period EMAs.

The MACD for a particular trading day is computed by subtracting the 26-period EMA from the 12-period

EMA. The resulting MACDs are plotted on the price chart and connected to create a MACD line.

Next, a 9-period EMA of the MACD, a.k.a., the signal line, is computed and plotted on top of or below the existing MACD line. The MACD line functions as a buying or selling trigger for traders. When the MACD line crosses to below the signal line, it's a signal for traders to take a short position on a security, i.e., to sell it. When the MACD line crosses above the signal line, it's a trigger for them to take a long position on a security, i.e., buy it.

When the 12-period EMA is higher than the 26-period one, the MACD's value is considered positive, which is usually colored blue in computer-plotted charts. When the 12-period EMA's lower than the 26-period EMA, the value's negative and is usually colored red. The farther the MACD is above or below the baseline, the greater the gap between the two EMAs is.

Often times, MACD is shown with a histogram that shows how wide the gaps are between the signal line and the MACD. The histogram is above the MACD baseline when the MACD is above the signal line and below the baseline if the MACD is below the signal line.

Traders can estimate the strength of trend momentums through the MACD histogram.

Traders use the MACD indicator in a couple of ways. One is through crossovers. As mentioned earlier, traders sell their securities when the MACD crosses to below the 9-day EMA signal line. Conversely, traders take positions in or buy securities when the MACD crosses to above the signal line. But because the MACD isn't a perfect trading system, many traders wait to confirm such crossings over before taking or unloading positions in securities to minimize the risks of unprofitable trades.

MACD crossovers tend to be more accurate when they correspond to current prevailing trends. When the MACD crosses above the signal line after a short correction phase during a long-term bullish trend, they can be interpreted as confirmations of a bullish sentiment on securities. But when MACDs go below the signal line after a short spike during a long-term down trend, they can be interpreted as a confirmation of a bearish sentiment.

Another way traders use the MACD is through divergence. To be specific, divergence refers to when the MACD's highs or lows deviate from the related highs and lows of the security's price. When the security's MACD forms two increasing lows that correspond to two decreasing lows of a security's price, it's called a bullish divergence. This is considered by many traders as a valid bullish signal for a long-term bull market, which may be taken to mean as a position-taking signal for swing trading.

When the MACD creates two consecutive falling highs while the security's high prices go up for two consecutive periods, it's considered as a bearish divergence. When it appears during an ongoing bear market, it's interpreted as a confirmation that the bear market will most likely persist. Thus, it can be treated as a sign to either liquidate a position or wait further until taking a swing trading position on a security.

Quick falls and rises in the MACD can also indicate possible changes in buying or selling pressure or momentum of a security, i.e., an impending change in trend. In particular, sharp rises and falls can indicate overbought and oversold positions, both of which indicate possible reversal of a trend and opportunities to swing trade. In this regard, traders often use the MACD with the RSI or relative strength index.

While the MACD and RSI both indicate whether a security is overbought or oversold, they're different in one aspect. RSI price changes while MACD uses the difference between two exponential moving averages or EMAs. Because they both indicate whether a security is overbought or oversold using different parameters, traders often use them together for a more complete analysis of securities' buying or selling pressure.

MACD isn't a perfect indicator, too. One of the challenges of using MACD relates to divergence. In particular, it can produce trend reversal signals that don't result in actual reversals, which are also called as "false positives." Also, can also fail to identify actual reversals.

On-Balance Volume (OBV)

Trading volume can give traders insights on how the general investing public feels about a security, i.e., bearish or bullish, especially in conjunction with price chart patterns. Unusually high trading volume during significant price drops or spikes may confirm trend reversals or continuations, depending on the price action. Accumulation-distribution indicators help interpret market sentiment through trading volume with greater accuracy than simply looking at trading volume alone.

On-Balance Volume or OBV is a technical indicator developed during the 1960s, which totals up and down volumes and adds or subtracts their results continuously to create smoother volume indicating lines that are akin to price bars or charts. These lines make it easier to analyze volume trends together with price trends for more accurate swing trading signals.

OBV provides a highly accurate way of confirming major price peaks and troughs, which make them an ideal tool for estimating potential price spikes or drops.

Using OBV is simple: just compare the OBVs movement to that of a security's prices, paying close attention to convergences or divergences between the two.

The following are some of the ways the two interact, including what they mean:

The OBV reaching a new peak as the security's price tests an established resistance level indicates a bullish divergence. This signifies a high probability that the security's price will breach the established resistance level and surge upward.

The security's price reaching a new peak as its OBV tests an established resistance level indicates a bearish divergence. This signifies a high probability that an upward trend will either pause or reverse soon.

The OBV dropping to a new low as the security's price tests an established support level indicates a bearish divergence. This signifies a high probability that the security's price will breach the support and drop even further.

The security's price hitting a new low while its OBV tests an established support level indicates a bullish divergence. It signifies that the security price's downtrend may either pause or reverse soon.

On Choosing Technical Indicators

Choosing technical indicators to use, especially as a newbie swing trader, can be overwhelming. Fortunately, it's something that can be done well by choosing any or all of the above-mentioned popular technical indicators. They're some of the most popular for very good reasons, some of which include practicality and accuracy.

How to use each Technical Analysis (Indicators) for swing trading

One of the first thing that beginning traders are going to notice is that there are a nearly endless number of indicators. Some are better than others, but you can end up getting lost in the forest by getting too absorbed in indicators and the various options available. The reality, however, is that piling on more and more indicators isn't going to give you more information. So its actually better to settle on a small number of indicators that you can use to help determine your trading moves.

Simple Moving Averages

The first thing that you might notice when looking at a stock market chart is that it doesn't really have any resemblance to a smooth mathematical curve. Its jagged and messy, even if you can tease out trends and shapes out of the constant price changes. Wouldn't it be nice if we could eliminate the noise? And maybe that would help us zoom in on trends and possible changes in trends.

That's exactly what a moving average seeks to accomplish. A moving average is a smoothed out curve that has gotten rid of all the noise. If you have a moving average with a period of x, that moving average will sum up the prices from the previous x days, and then divide by the total number of days used in the average. It's called moving because at each day it's recalculated, so it incorporates new pricing as it moves from left to right across the chart. In the next section we'll look at more complicated moving averages that can give us better information, but for now we will stick to simple moving averages.

Most of the time, you will use a moving average based on the closing price for each time step on your chart. However, you could also use the opening price, the volume of trading, and the high price for the day, the low price for the day, plus some more complicated averages that try to give you the full information for each trading day.

For example, HLC is going to include the average of the high, low, and close for each trading day. So at each day, it will calculate the HLC for the day, and then the moving average will be the averages of the HLC's calculated at each point.

This can be carried out further, using OHLC, which also includes the opening price. That way the entire pricing information for the day is incorporated into the average – you can even think about this as taking the averages of the candles, since they include this information.

However, you'll find that the curves usually match up pretty well, so simply using a closing moving average is probably going to be all you need to do. However, the beauty of these tools is that trading websites have all of them built-in, and so you don't have to worry about the mathematical details of what's behind the calculations.

More important that picking which item to track (other than volume, as swing traders we want to focus on price and try to deduce pricing trends and reversals) is the number of periods used to compute the moving average. The chart below, which shows IBM stock for the past 12 months, makes this pretty clear. The red line in the center is a 10 period simple moving average. Notice that it gives use a nice match to the actual stock prices, providing a smoothed out curve that follows the actual stock prices pretty well. Below this you see two curves – or maybe you can't make them out. One is the 50 period moving average using closing price, the other is the 50 period moving average using OHLC, showing that at least in this case, using OHLC doesn't add any additional information.

Looking for cross overs

One of the most important ways that a trader will use moving averages is to look for crossovers. In particular, you're looking for the shorter period moving average to cross above or below the longer period moving average. When this happens, it can indicate a true reversal. You can see that in the IBM chart. When the short term trend (red) crosses below the long term trend lines, the stock is in a downtrend. The relative positions of the lines don't change when there are retracements. When the short term line crosses above the long period average, then that signals an uptrend, and we see that in the chart.

Typically traders will use 20 period and 50 period moving averages, or even 200 period moving averages. Here we see a clearer picture when using the 20 and 50 period moving averages for the IBM chart:

Simple moving averages, while they can provide a lot of useful information, have one defect. That is they give equal weight to prices from long ago and to recent prices. In order to spot shorter term price trends, it can be more useful to weight the prices, giving more weight to recent priced and less weight to prices that happened in the past.

Exponential moving averages

This is what many more advanced moving averages do for you. Exponential moving averages, which weight prices to eliminate the weakness of giving equal reliance to older prices, are very popular among day traders and Forex traders. The chart below shows Apple with a 20 day and 50 day moving average. Note that both nicely follow the actual prices. More to the point, the crossovers more accurately indicate changing trends in price.

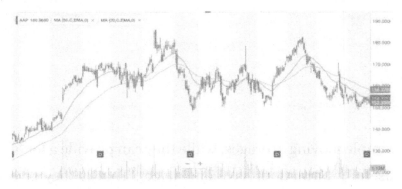

So how can this be used in practice? Traders often like to use a 50 day and a 200 day moving average to spot reversals. The charts are nice and pretty when looking back on them. Let's take a look at January 1 through February 15 for Tesla. It looked like this:

Note the cross over point – the 50 day moving average crossed below the 200 day moving average. This kind of crossover is called a "death cross". To see why, we just have to extend the Tesla chart out for the next 5 months, and we see it entered a long downturn.

When you are doing your analysis, you may want to use moving averages with different periods, but always pick a moving average with a short period and one with a long period.

Another crossing to look for when considering charts with a 50 day moving average and a 200 day moving average is called the "golden cross". This indicates a coming uptrend. Here we see SNAP:

Zooming out to show what followed, the indicator proved correct.

Bollinger Bands

Finding points where true reversals can occur is important, but so is locating levels of support and resistance. Bollinger bands can be added to your stock charts and help you determine what these price ranges are. Note that Bollinger bands are dynamic, so each day the level of support and resistance is going to be adjusted. But this will give you a more accurate picture of what's going on rather than just relying on drawing straight lines through the charts.

Bollinger bands have three parts. The middle part is a simple moving average, by default it gives you a 20 period moving average. The upper band is 2 standard deviations above the moving average, and it helps you to identify the zone of resistance. The lower band is two standard deviations below the moving average, and so helps you identify support. Here we added Bollinger bands to the SNAP chart, keeping the exponential moving averages so that we can see the point of the golden cross. We've also denoted some interesting candles.

When you see stock prices on the edge of the Bollinger bands that indicates that the prices are over bought or oversold, because they are one or two standard deviations from the mean. However that doesn't mean a trend reversal is coming. On the left side of the chart, notice that two of the candles actually fall outside the Bollinger bands – and so they are more than two standard deviations away from the 20 day mean. And indeed, after that there was a short term decline in prices. However that seems to be more of a retracement. The golden cross held true and the stock has continued to climb.

If you look at the first dotted oval, you will see that the bottom candle also falls outside the range of the Bollinger bands. That would be an excellent buying point for the stock. It was followed by a strong upturn.

Don't blindly make trading moves when you see prices fall outside the Bollinger band. Use multiple indicators to look for the trend and trade with the trend.

One thing to look for is the width of the Bollinger bands. If they get wide, that is telling you that the stock is gaining more volatility. When they are tightening, that means there is less volatility, but that can be followed by large breakouts to one side or the other.

Looking at Netflix, we can see that this kind of phenomenon might be setting up:

Narrow bands - less volatility, closer to the mean. Coming breakout?

Wide bands - more volatility

Look for narrow bands because a breakout move is possible in the future. Volatility can expand after a period of narrow bands.

One of the ways that you can use Bollinger bands is to look for opportunities to enter trades. If you are looking for the stock price to increase, you can wait for it to hit the lower Bollinger band, or even to fall slightly below it. If you can confirm with signals of a coming uptrend, this can be a good opportunity to buy, with a trigger to sell at the level of the upper Bollinger band.

Sometimes the stock will be trading above or below the mean, but you'll see it reverting to the mean as it goes up and down. Although these represent smaller opportunities to profit, when it reverts to the mean this could be a buying opportunity, and then you look for it to rise again to hit the upper Bollinger band, and sell at that point.

Alternatively you could short the stock at the top and wait for it to revert to the mean on the way back down.

When the security is in a big trend, you can use the 20 period moving average to set your stop-loss. In this example, Apple is making a big move up in price, and you can see all the candles are well above the mean.

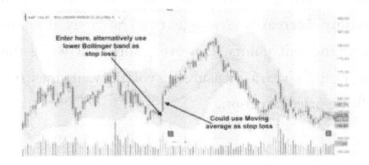

Following the strong uptrend, we see an equally strong downtrend. Notice how closely the candles in both cases are following the outer Bollinger bands.

True Range and Average True Range

True range is calculated at each trading day (or point you are using) and is taken to the largest of one of the three following quantities:

- Difference between the current days high price and its low price
- The difference between the previous days closing price and the current days high price
- The difference between yesterdays closing price and todays low price

This is a measure of volatility in the share price. It can then be averaged using a 14 day moving average to give the average true range. Average true range increases with increasing volatility and decreases with when volatility decreases. Average true range is used to determine exit points. However, note that while the true range gives a measure of volatility, it does not indicate price direction.

The Chandelier exit uses true range to calculate an exit point by calculating a multiple of the true range, then subtracting that from the highest high that occurred after entering the trade. So it would define a stop loss point, typically using 3 x the average true range subtracted from the high.

ADX and Moving Average Convergence/Divergence (MACD)

Directional movement indices are a way to measure the momentum that bulls or bears have in the market. However these usually aren't used alone, instead the difference between the two, which is called the ADX is used to measure the strength of a trend. In the chart below, we see the ADX is plotted below the Apple year to date stock chart. The ADX shows the strength of the trend with positive being an upward trend since it's the difference between the directional movement indexes for bulls pushing prices above the previous days high minus the directional movement index for bears. Bulls are indicated by the green line and bears by the red line.

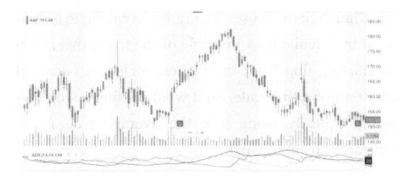

The way that a trader will use the ADX, is to confirm that a real trend exists. Of course in this example we have picked an obvious trend to highlight, but not all trends are that obvious, but you can confirm by looking for movement in the ADX. Entry and exit points can be selected by looking for cross overs in the directional movement indices. When the bullish index crosses over the bearish line that is a buy signal if you are long on the stock. To sell, you would look for the green line crossing back below the red line. When shorting stock, you'd look for the red line crossing the green line, indicating that a downward trend was beginning. You can see the from the chart that these are accurately reflected in the actual trends that occurred, so they make one of the best tools you can use for determining when to enter or exit a trade.

MACD is a trend following indicator based on exponential moving averages. It takes the 12 period moving average and then subtracts the 26 period moving average. The MACD includes a signal line and when it crosses above the signal line, this is taken as a buy signal if you are hoping for a rise in stock price. When it crosses below the signal line that is a sell signal (reverse if shorting the stock). In the chart below we have used the MACD with the chart for Apple stock.

Choose your indicators

As we mentioned above, drowning yourself in multiple indicators is probably not going to be very productive. The best approach to use is to pick 2 or 3 and stick with them. The MACD is one of the most effective indicators, but simply looking for cross overs between short and long period moving averages works quite well. You can combine this with looking at candles to make effective buy and sell decisions. But remember this is not a precise science and the fact that people's behavior and the stock market in general are chaotic, and also impacted by news often quite dramatically, means not all of your trades are going to work despite using every tool that is available. The only thing you can really accomplish is tipping the odds in your favor, so that you end up with more wins than losses. The point here is you shouldn't get too down when trades go bad.

Moving Averages

Moving averages is a great tool that help you to determine the direction of a trend and also to quickly spot indicators that signify a change in the trend. There are lots of details about moving averages (how they are computed and constructed) that will not interest a beginner to swing trading. At best, they will simply bore you! One rule of thumb I would recommend to you as a beginner is to always look out for simplicity.

When something becomes too complex, there is a greater chance of failing at it. So I will not bother you with the computational details of moving averages. You may wish to look them up and get acquainted with them after you become good at swing trading. For now, let us give our focus to this one main fact about moving averages: the line of a moving average indicates a stock's average price over a given period. It is that simple.

Basically, two types of moving averages have become very popular over the years and are commonly used by traders. They are SMA – Simple Moving Average, and the EMA – Exponential Moving Average. These can easily be used to identify likely resistance and support levels (more on support and resistance later).

Simple Moving Averages versus Exponential Moving Averages

The simple moving averages (SMA) are glaringly dissimilar from the exponential moving averages (EMA). However, that does not translate into one being superior to the other. Simple moving averages depict a more precise reflection of price average for a whole period. This is why the simple moving averages are considered well-tailored for determining support and resistance level of a trend. On the flip side, the exponential moving averages are characterized by less lag. This makes them more responsive to changes in price that occur more recently. This means that exponential moving averages are sure to move well ahead of the simple moving averages.

Simple Moving Average (SMA)

Daily Chart - Dow Jones Industrial Average ETF (DIA)

Buy

Buy Buy

Buy Buy

Buy

Buy

Simple Moving Average (20-day)

1. Established Uptrend
2. Stock Price falls below Moving Average
3. Buy when Price Closes above Moving Average

Commodity.com - all rights reserved

You could experiment with any of the two and find what works well for you. However, you also have the choice of combining the two on a single chart. And we will see how to do just that.

How to Use Both Averages

Combining the simple moving averages with the exponential moving averages is a good way to maximize their benefits. Let us take a look at how to combine the two in the following example.

In this example, I shall use the 10-period SMA in combination with the 30-period EMA. One good advantage of combining a fast and a slow moving average is because once the fast average crosses the slow one, it is a high indicator of a possible change in trend. Take a look at this example.

The chart above is pretty simple to read. The 10-period SMA is positioned just above the 30 EMA in August while the trend is up. But as the 10-period SMA crosses down in mid-August, the trend also drops down. Notice that by mid-September there is still another cross by the 10-period SMA above the 30 EMA and the trend went back up and remains that way for a long time.

From the above we can deduce the following (pay close attention if you choose to use the 10-period SMA in combination with the 30-period EMA):

When the 10-period SMA is above the 30-period EMA your trading emphasis should be ongoing long.

When the 10-period SMA is below the 30-period EMA your trading emphasis should be ongoing short.

I am keeping this as simple as possible because I know this is a beginner's guide. What you need is the essentials, and that is what I am focused upon. Going into the nitty-gritty will spoil the fun for you as a beginner. Stick to the simple strategies for now and you will make good progress.

Please note:

Moving averages work well when applied to trending stocks. When a stock is in the trading ranges phase, moving averages will do you no good.

It is vital that there should be wide spaces between the two moving averages.

The 10-period SMA has to be above the 30-period EMA before you go for long positions.

The 10-period SMA has to be below the 30-period EMA before you go for short positions.

It is compulsory for the two moving averages to slop upwards before you go for long positions.

It is compulsory for the two moving averages to slop downwards before you go for short positions.

Moving Averages: Advantages

Here are some of the advantages that come with using moving averages.

1. Moving averages helps you to easily build your skills to identify great openings for making good trades.

2. It helps you to trade in the direction of dominant market trends so that you can easily beat the odds.

3. It is a very simple method to identify market trends and the possibility of a breakout.

4. It provides a simple visual depiction of the prevailing market trend and the general price action of a specific time frame.

Moving Averages: Disadvantages

As with all things that have advantages, there is sure to be some disadvantages. Here are a few disadvantages of using the moving averages.

1. There could be a possible false signal in the case of abrupt rise or fall in the price of a stock.

2. It only gives you a general overview of the trend plus the likely entry and exit points. However, you must be ready to make the call for the exact spot you wish to enter or exit a trade in a way that is beneficial for you.

3. Depending on the average charting, it can generate noise.

4. To get a good idea of the market position, the time period is very critical.

Testing Price Boundaries

One other important use of moving averages is to determine support and resistance areas on a chart. The support and resistance are basically the limits or boundaries against which the rising and falling price movements of a stock are tested. The more often there is an attempted breach against these boundaries, the more likely there will be a breakout or a change in the direction of the trend (more about support and resistance in the next section).

Bottom Line

Moving averages are a great market tool, but you must always have it in mind that they are a lagging indicator.

Their function is mainly to confirm a trend that has been established already. You cannot use moving averages to accurately predict a trend. Nevertheless, you can use them as a yardstick to evaluate future movements in price.

How to use indicators from the Moves of Big Players

What is relative strength? The Relative Strength Indicator is a technical indicator that measures the strength or momentum of any gains and losses made by stock based on the closing price. These are often shown or indicated on candlestick charts over a given period of time. This helps traders to determine whether the stock has been oversold or overbought.

There is a simple formula for calculating the relative strength index. Relative strength is obtained by dividing the average gain with the average loss. The RSI or relative strength index calculation is determined based on 14 periods of time. There are important factors about this popular index. Here they are.

The relative strength index is quite popular with traders and they use it to make an analysis on different markets such as the stocks, commodities, and money markets.

The index is ideally a momentum oscillator which measures the size and direction of price movement relating to specific stocks.

Momentum of stocks as the RSI index is calculated as the ratio of higher closes to lower closes. This basically means that should there be more candlesticks that close with higher gains, then the RSI will increase in value. But if there are candlesticks with lower gains, then the RSI will decrease in value.

The RSI lies on a scale from 1 to 100. Traders commonly prefer to use two distinct levels. These are the 30 and 70 levels.

Information Revealed by the RSI Index

When the RSI index is below 30, it simply means that the price is weak and has been on a downward trend.

If the index is below the 30 value and is in the oversold area, this might mean the price is close to reversal.

However, when the index is above the 70 level mark, then it is a strong indicator that the price has been performing quite well and is really strong.

But if the RSI index is above 70 and in the area indicating a share has been over purchased, then the price may be due for a reversal.

Simple Ways of Trading the RSI Indicator

There are about 3 basic ways of trading stocks using the relative strength indicator. These are listed below.

1. Trade stocks when the index is in the oversold area. This means to buy more stock.

2. Trade the markets if the RSI index is within the overbought region. This translates to selling your stock.

3. Trade anytime you notice a divergence of the index. This basically implies that the RSI index and the share price are trending in opposing directions. As such, you are likely to notice the price going for higher highs yet on the indicator window the RSI will be on a lower high. This kind of behavior is also known as a divergence.

Trading an RSI in the Oversold Region

This is a pretty straightforward technique. What you need to do is confirm that the market is on a downward trend. Now check whether the RSI index has crossed below the 30-mark level because this is a good indicator that it is not in the oversold region so there is a high probability the price will start to head back up.

So for now, simply wait for the RSI line to head towards the 30 level region and then past it. Once the 30-mark level is surpassed, then you can proceed to purchase the relevant stock.

Trading an RSI Index in the Overbought Region

This approach is the exact opposite of the previous one. Here, we first confirm that the market is already on an upward trend. Now check to see that the RSI index has already crossed over and above the 70-mark level.

This will be a clear indicator the stock has entered the overbought region with potential for the price to begin a downward trend. Once this becomes obvious, simply sit back and wait for the RSI to begin its downturn at least until it touches the 70-mark level. Once this level is surpassed, then you are free to sell the stock.

Selling or Trading on an RSI Index Divergence

If you are too successfully and profitably sell on the RSI divergence, then you need to be able to notice the sell trading setup then purchase the trading setup once it begins to form. First, ensure that the RSI oscillator line is clearly and well over the 70-mark level. This is a necessary condition if you are to trade the RSI divergence.

During an upward trend, the price of the stock should show a high that corresponds to a similar high by the RSI indicator. However, you are likely to observe the RSI index when the price gets to the next higher high. When this happens then you will receive the information that RSI divergence has occurred with the potential of a price increase so be ready to sell your stock.

Tips on How to Use the RSI Effectively

When there are sudden price movements in the stock market, false sell or buy signals can be generated on the index. Therefore, avoid using it on its own and instead use other indicators as well to confirm whether the signals are genuine or not.

There are traders who, instead of using additional markers, choose to apply quite extreme values of the RSI ratio. These are used as the sell or buy signals, for instance, readings above 80 or below 20. The figures above 80 are supposed to indicate an overbuy situation while the figure below 20 is meant to indicate an oversell situation.

This index is sometimes used together with trend lines because the trend line resistance and support often point to resistance and support levels of the RSI index. As a trader, you need to be on the lookout for convergence or divergence that occurs between the RSI indicator and the stock price. This is yet another reliable way of making use of the indicator.

Ideally, divergence takes place whenever a stock hits a new high or low in its price without the RSI index making a corresponding new low or high value. There are both bearish and bullish points of divergence.

A bearish divergence can be described as the situation where the price makes a new high while the RSI index does. This divergence is viewed as a sell signal. On the other hand, a bullish divergence occurs when the price of a stock hits a new but the RSI index does not do so. This is then considered as a purchase signal.

Take the example of a stock that sees an increase in price to $50. Now the RSI index goes to indicate a high reading of 65. Then the stock experiences a slight retraction in the downward direction. The stock then goes on to hit a new height of $55 while the RSI gets to only 60. This shows that the RSI has diverged and taken a bearish position and has generally diverged from the price movement.

The Downside of the Relative Strength Indicator

Every indicator has its benefits and downside. While the RSI index is a great indicator when trading the markets, there are chances that price tops and price bottoms can occur much later after the overbought and oversold zones are reached. This means that when an RSI is below the 30-mark level in the oversold region, there is no guarantee that once this happens the price will start going up.

Also, the indicator can stay in the overbought or oversold region for a much longer period of time especially in a strong trending market. This can give a false buy or sell signal. It is advisable, therefore, to use more indicators to confirm the necessary trades. You can use charts and other indicators mentioned above.

Learn and Benefit From Moves of the Big Players

Big investors may not agree on much but they do generally agree that generating big profits in the markets needs a relentless strategy and plan that revolves around a solid set of rules. A lot of beginners and small-time traders jump into the market with very little knowledge of the markets. Most of the time you sold too early, probably didn't understand what terms such as spread mean and so on.

Support and Resistance

Take a good look at a chart. You'll notice there are some areas that buyers appear to be more dominant. This is known as demand because the buyers are significantly dominating the market, making the price of the stock to rise. Certainly, if everyone is trying to buy a particular stock at the same time, it makes sense for the price to go up. When the demand for a stock is high, it shows up on a chart as support.

On the other hand, there are some areas on the chart where you'll notice that sellers are more in control. This is what is known as supply because the sellers are rushing out of their positions in the market, making the price of the stock they are selling to drop. Of course, when everyone is selling a stock, the value has nowhere to go but down. When the supply for a stock is high it shows up on a chart as resistance.

All of this simply means that support and resistance are key indicators for helping traders find out areas of demand and supply. Therefore, as a smart swing trader, the most sensible thing for you to do is to buy stocks during periods you have identified as support.

Why you should do this is because, in all likelihood, traders who purchased the stock at the dying minute and then began to witness a downtrend in the stock will want to leave that position by breaking even. So they are likely to rush into selling.

And on the flip side, it is obvious you should sell the stocks during the periods you have identified as resistance. This is because many traders who did not get in on time while the stock was heading up have seen another opportunity and are most likely to rush into buying.

Nevertheless, you must be careful about buying at support and selling at resistance. Be sure to use more than one analysis tool before you attempt this so as not to encounter monumental failure. Remember, nothing is a hundred percent sure in trading stocks.

What Novices Do Not Know

Furthermore, be aware that there are several types of support and resistance.

Looking at this from the long angle, a stock that drops back to a previous low is more worthy of your attention than a stock that drops back to a previous high.

Equally, from the short angle, a stock that moves up to a previous high should get more of your attention than a stock that moves up to a previous low.

But do you know what most novice traders do? They buy stocks when the stocks are running into resistance (when there is supply). And they sell their stock when it falls into support (when there is demand). This is completely backward and does not give you any meaningful profits from trading. For you to make money from swing trading, you should identify early when there is a period that presents an opportunity to buy and also the early signals to sell. Let the novices come in later after the major buying has been done and let them sell when the major selling is already over.

Smart swing traders are always on the lookout to make profits from novices because they are always there to buy from you (when there should be selling) and sell to you (when they should be buying). You have an edge because you are not guessing or following the crowd. You are implementing a perfectly laid out plan to make a profit. Your investment in acquiring the right trading knowledge will pay off if implemented correctly.

Tips on Profiting from Support and Resistance

Now, let us look at a few tips on how you, a swing trader, can analyze the support and resistance levels of a stock chart to make good profits. Note that I am only referring to simple support and resistance in these tips. Support and resistance that occurs when a stock price falls or rises to touch a price level for a few days are referred to as simple support and resistance. When there is a repeated touch on a price level frequently, it is termed significant support and resistance level.

More often than not, simple support and resistance happen at whole or round numbers. So, as you analyze your stock chart, it is a good practice to note at what round numbers the stock is finding support or running into resistance.

Normally, horizontal lines on a chart can be used to define support and resistance levels. These lines will give you a visual representation of areas of aggressive buying and torrential selling. The slant trend lines on a downtrend can also be seen as a resistance level, and the inclined trend lines on an uptrend can also be seen as a support level.

Another trend line that may not be very obvious at first is the moving averages. Sometimes when there is a downtrend, you will find a moving average becoming a resistance level at the top of the falling prices. And on the flip side, it is not out of place to find moving averages below rising prices in an uptrend providing support.

When a resistance level is breached or broken, it is highly possible for the resistance to become the new support level.

When a support level is breached or broken, it is highly possible for the support to become the new resistance level.

What Indicators Mean to You as a Beginner

If you read most books on swing trading or trading in general, you will discover that indicators are somewhat sorted into two broad groups, namely: leading indicators and lagging indicators. While leading indicators are meant to lead price actions, lagging indicators follow price actions. These are awesome tools that can help an experienced trader. But you are a beginner at swing trading. The question you should be asking is how did these indicators come about? Leading indicators lead price action in what sense? Can there be any indicator drawn on a chart without a price action preceding it? Does that not effectively make the so-called leading indicator an actual lagging indicator when it comes to real-life application? Think about it.

The reason I bring this up, is to let you as a beginner take a breather from racking your brain in a bid to understand some of the complexities of technical indicators. Realize that whatever a technical indicator will tell you is right in front of you as a chart. So your first indicator is the chart. Learn how to read stock charts, and you would have learned a great deal even without a technical indicator.

You have learned the following:

- Volumes on a stock chart tell you the interest level of traders on a particular stock.
- The liquidity or illiquidity of a stock shows up on the volume.
- Moving averages help you to quickly spot early signals for a change in the direction of a trend.

- SMA and EMA can be combined to give a better reading.
- Moving averages works better with trending stocks not trading ranges.
- Moving averages are lagging indicators, meaning they only confirm an already established trend.
- Demand means buyers are dominating a stock within a given time frame. This causes the price to go up.
- Supply means sellers are leaving their positions making prices to fall.
- Support and resistance levels help you to identify areas of demand and supply.
- Once broken, there is a high chance of support or resistance becoming the other.
- Trend lines and moving averages can also be seen as support and resistance levels.

Smart swing traders usually buy at a support level and sell at a resistance level. However, be careful when buying at a support because it could also tank! Remember, there are no 100 percent guarantees in trading stocks no matter the methods utilized.

Learn to Separate Substance from Fluff

As a trader, you need to be able to filter out market noise. This is an essential requirement if you are to succeed and make big money investing in the stock market. You also need to take the three important actions of investing. These are;

- Zeroing in on volume and price action
- Focus closely on a stock's fundamentals and chart activity
- Ignore just about everything else
- Things you should ignore

There are certain bits and pieces of information that you should not pay heed to. For instance, if a friend or relative reveals that a certain firm is about to receive a government contract, then you should ignore such information. It should be treated as a rumor and not factual information.

A columnist or commentator may claim that a potential investment is not worth your time simply because they have concerns that have no history on stock activity. Such thoughts are not well reasoned and should, therefore, be ignored. Even information from analysts that have not been properly analyzed should be treated like noise and ignored.

Instead, you should do what big investors often do. They study stocks and listen to the markets in silence. You can also study the actions of big investors and observe what it is that they do. For instance, search and find out which fund owned what stock and whether a particular trend in ownership tends downwards or upwards.

Watch Fund Managers

Lots of the time, market analysts and columnists are often ignored even when they offer their opinions on TV and elsewhere. Basically, fund managers are the experts to watch because their actions determine the outcome of trades at the markets. For instance, they will never talk bad about a stock but will sell it. Also, they never unnecessarily praise a stock but instead, they invest in it. Therefore, watch their actions and learn from what they do.

Watch Major Stocks

You should also watch the activity of major stocks and shares. You can find this information readily available on different websites and platforms. Sometimes the information shows which funds hold which stocks and in what quantity. This kind of information is very important and helps to ensure that you are in the know about what stocks can move the markets in a big way.

Have your Own Set of Investing Rules

As a trader, you should craft your own rules that will guide you as you trade and invest in the stock market. You can start by asking successful investors what type of rules they followed, what their investment policies or principles that they followed to be so successful. Here are some policies that will guide you when you are looking to buy and invest in stocks.

1. Be patient with winning trades and impatient with losing trades.

This is a great rule to live by, declared by Dennis Gartman, who often advises hedge fund managers, mutual funds, trading firms, and brokerage firms. He is also an accomplished trader and regular commenter on finance networks. According to Mr. Gartman, it is very possible to make plenty of money if you are correct 30% of the time so long as profits are large and losses small.

This rule also advises on a couple of other mistakes that traders often make. For instance, a trader is likely to sell at the first sign of profit. Instead, Gartman advises to let a winning trade continue its run. Also, traders should not allow a losing trade to get away. Investors are generally okay with losing a little bit of money but not a lot of it. Remember, therefore, that you do not have to be right most of the time. Remember too, that it is okay to lose a little bit of money but not a lot.

2. It is better to buy into a wonderful company at a fair price than buy a fair company at a wonderful price.

This is a great rule followed by Warren Buffett. Warren is considered as the most successful stock market investor in history. He is one of the richest men in the world and has advised numerous US presidents. And whenever Warren talks, the markets listen. His letters and teachings to his investment firm are used by top business schools to teach finance students.

Buffett offers two crucial pieces of advice. One is, when investing in a company, always look at its fundamentals. This means listening to conference calls, observing the balance sheets and having confidence in the firm's management. The second piece of advice is to only look at the price and evaluate it once the quality of the company has been affirmed. Traders should not expect to buy shares of a quality company at throwaway prices but at fair, market value prices. Also, do not buy the shares of a poorly performing company even if they are priced really low.

3. If you really like a stock, then put at least 10% of your money into it

This is advice that's been put forward by Bill Gross. Bill is one of the founders of PIMCO which is the among the world's biggest bond funds on the globe. His statement above speaks mostly about investment rather than trading. According to Bill, you really should diversify your portfolio and never put all your money in one box.

As an investor, you also have to take chances in the market based on well-informed research. Also, always have some cash in your accounts to fund those trades that may require a little more capital.

What is mean reversion trading?

The term "mean reversion trading" is also known as the counter-trend or simply reversal trading? In this kind of trade, you will be looking for stock prices that have shifted significantly away from the mean price. Essentially, the mean reversion strategy seeks unsustainable trends.

To calculate the mean price of a commodity or stock, use the moving average and then apply it to the charts. If you observe the charts closely, you will notice that the price attempts a reversion to numerous times but failed. This means that the mean reversion strategy is more than just a trading towards the moving average. This kind of trade requires risk management approach, a very strict entry management and an emotionally stable investor who will not over trade or seek revenge trading.

Summary of Technical Analysis – Indicator Tools

With the advent and then increased use of computers over the past decades, a wide range of different technical analyses has become much more accessible to every individual Retail trader. Imagine how labor intensive it would have been 25 years ago to sit down with a pencil, paper and calculator to plot out an average comprised of 200 numbers. How about 50 years ago, doing it with a slide rule?

Today, many Institutional trading firms are using computers to make purchase and sale decisions on different markets. These computers run "algorithms" (essentially a computer program) that monitor price and volume, perform ongoing technical analysis, and then make actual trades based on the results of that analysis. The programmers design the algorithms to perform functions at a certain point or technical event. One can imagine the impact that these algorithms might have if a number of different firms were all running programs with similar action parameters. Moves would certainly be somewhat predictable.

There are now hundreds of different technical studies that are readily available to all traders and machines. These studies analyze and attempt to predict stock price movements. Below is a short list of some commonly used technical studies:

- Moving averages (simple and exponential)
- Support and resistance lines
- Momentum indicators
- Trading patterns

Because machines and their algorithms make technical analysis ever more important today, these studies are very useful to swing traders, and essentially create self-fulfilling events. In other words, an expectation about a stock price movement event can affect the buying group's behavior toward that movement, which will then cause the expectation to be realized.

As an example, traders and machines that do technical analysis commonly watch a 20-day simple moving average of a stock's price. When a stock's price is on the rise, the 20-day moving average price will follow along on the uptrend, while remaining under the current price. Let's assume there is some profit-taking and the stock starts to drop. Unless there is some fundamental reason for the change in attitude toward the stock, people and machines wait at the 20-day moving average price to buy. When the stock hits that price or close to it, the buyers come in and the price rebounds, continuing to reinforce that the 20-day moving average event is almost always an area of support.

The large number of studies now available for use by traders can be overwhelming and leave you to wonder which one or ones you should use. I suggest that you find a couple of tools that you feel comfortable using and then focus on them rather than getting bogged down with trying to manage and find alignment with too many indicators.

- Support and resistance levels
- Moving averages (simple and exponential)
- Relative Strength Index (RSI)
- MACD: convergence and divergence
- Average True Range (ATR)

After reading and studying this section, you will have some excellent tools to use to identify trading opportunities. There are also many other swing trading tools available, so I encourage you to continue looking at other measures as you further develop your trading skills and strategies.

Support and Resistance Levels

Now that you understand the candlestick and how it shows price action in the market for a stock, I will examine how support and resistance levels can be used to predict future price movements in a stock. This is one of the easiest forms of charting and does not require any formulas or complicated calculations. All you need is your eyes and a small amount of creativity.

When stocks move up, they tend to find price levels that are hard to break through. For stocks heading higher, these levels are called areas of resistance. Conversely, stocks that are dropping will eventually find price levels where buyers come in and prevent the price from moving lower. These are called areas of support. If you look at a chart that contains a series of candlesticks over a long period of time, you should be able to identify where these areas of support and resistance occur. You can do this for a 1-hour chart, a daily chart or even a weekly chart. Sometimes these support and resistance levels are common to all time frames.

Horizontal support or resistance trading is simple but very effective. My years of trading experience have shown and taught us that the market remembers price levels, which is why these support or resistance lines make sense. You might ask - why does the marketplace remember these levels? Again, it is a self-fulfilling prophecy. Most of the knowledgeable traders and machines are looking at the same charts and drawing the same lines and they all arrive at roughly the same values for support and resistance. So naturally, when one of those price levels is reached, there is additional buying or selling pressure depending on whether it is an area of support or resistance. Minor support or resistance areas will often cause price trends to pause. Major areas of support or resistance will often cause the prices to at least temporarily reverse.

Support is a price level where buying is strong enough to interrupt or reverse a downtrend. When a downtrend hits a support level, it bounces. Support is represented in a chart by a horizontal line connecting 2 or more bottoms. Resistance is a price level where selling is strong enough to interrupt or reverse an uptrend. Resistance is represented in a chart by a horizontal line connecting 2 or more tops.

Figure 8.1 and Figure 8.2 shown below illustrate how levels of support and resistance can clearly be seen on the daily charts of the SPDR S&P 500 ETF (SPY) and Sun Life Financial Inc. (SLF). Identifying these past levels can give you a clear indication of where future price levels will either bounce or be rejected.

Listed below are a number of items that you should be aware of when drawing support or resistance lines in hourly, daily or weekly charts:

The more recent levels of support or resistance are more relevant in comparison to levels that are from further in the past.

Levels of support or resistance that are tested often are stronger than levels only tested once and therefore they are harder to break through.

Look for individual indecision candles in the area of support or resistance because that is where the buyers and sellers are fighting to take control. An engulfing candle or doji at support or resistance will help confirm a possible price action reversal.

Often half-dollar ($0.50) and whole dollar numbers act as a support or resistance level, especially in lower than $10.00 stocks.

Support or resistance lines do not give you an exact price. They are more of an "area" where you will find this level. For example, if you drew a line in a stock chart and found an area of support at $21.20, you should not expect the price to go to and bounce exactly off of that $21.20 level. However, if you picked your line correctly, there is a good chance that somewhere around that level there will be some buying support. The stock might actually bounce at the $21.45 level or it could drop to $21.00 before bouncing back. Some factors that might affect the exact bounce level include overall market conditions on that day, the price of the stock (does it trade at $10.00 or $100.00 per share) and its Average True Range (how much the stock price varies day to day on average) to name a few.

The level of support or resistance should provide a very clear indication that it is in fact a level of support or resistance. If after reaching that price the stock flounders around that price level, and does not clearly reverse direction, then it may not be respecting that level. A common phrase is "the trend is your friend" – floundering around a price level will, more often than not, result in the price action continuing in the direction it was going initially.

If the price of a stock breaks through a level of resistance and continues higher, then that level of resistance now becomes a level of support if a downturn in price occurs. The same applies for down trending stocks that break a level of support. That level of support now becomes a resistance level should the stock turn and try to move higher.

Diagonal Lines

Some traders who work with charts also look for and rely on diagonal trend lines. You will typically find these in stocks and other financial instruments that are in long-term trends, either up or down. These can be useful because stocks never go straight up or down: they move in waves. These waves of price action can slowly move a stock up or down depending on whether the buyers or sellers are in control.

The challenge with diagonal waves is that they tend to be more subjective and open to interpretation by the creator. Other indicators like moving averages and momentum indicators can provide similar information but are not as open to interpretation by the chartist. This is why I prefer not to rely too heavily on any diagonal trendlines, however I am aware that numerous technical chart analysts do use them in assessing stocks that are trending higher or lower.

Diagonal lines can also be drawn in a stock that is either trending up or down to create a channel of trading in that trend. These diagonal channels of stocks in a long-term uptrend or downtrend can be used to keep you in a position for an extended period of time to maximize profits. You need to recognize that if you are using diagonal channels in this manner, your hold time may be much longer than a typical swing trade. Your trade could become a long-term hold and that may not be a bad thing if you are continuing to build wealth.

How to Use Support and Resistance Levels

Let's imagine you have a particular stock that during a scan has been identified as a potential long trade. You look at the chart and notice that the current price is close to a level of prior resistance. This is a price where it has not been able to break higher in the past. You would probably want to pass on going long on this stock because this is an area of prior price resistance.

Alternatively, if you find a stock that is trading just above a level of prior support, this may provide a good long entry from a risk to reward perspective. Your risk would be the price difference from the support level to the entry price. Next, you would look to find where you might expect the stock price to meet some resistance and then calculate your risk to reward ratio. Recall that your potential reward should be at least 2 times the risk you are taking on the trade.

Let's take a look at Figure 8.4 as an example of how you could have traded using levels of support and resistance. This daily chart of FireEye, Inc. (FEYE) clearly shows areas of support and resistance. The stock price fluctuates between these 2 levels giving opportunities to go long and to go short as shown in the figure. At the break of support in August, you would have quickly been stopped out or not have taken that trade at all due to the gap down and erratic price action.

The chart in Figure 8.4 also shows how support becomes resistance once the support is broken. There is a pause at the previous level of support before news related to the stock results in a gap and go price movement. The news was particularly good because the upper prior level of resistance did not stop the stock from moving higher after a very short pause.

Levels of support and resistance will often provide you with good reference prices for risk and reward calculations assuming you get the entry price in your trade plan. Having a good risk to reward ratio is crucial to your success as a trader.

Moving Averages

Moving averages are another very popular and relatively simple trading tool that can be used by a swing trader. They can assist you in getting a good entry on a stock and further help you to stay in a position to take advantage of a long-term trend. They can also provide a good signal for when you should make an exit.

Moving averages come in 2 primary types: simple and exponential. Both of these moving averages can be calculated using different periods of time. The longer the time period used, the more likely the average will lag behind a stock price in an uptrend or downtrend. Let's start by looking at the difference between the simple and exponential moving averages, and then look at different time periods, and then, finally, consider how best to use them with your swing trading strategies.

Simple vs. Exponential Moving Averages

The difference between the simple moving average (SMA) and the exponential moving average (EMA) can be significant and your choice of which one you choose to use can make an impact on your trading. An SMA is calculated by starting with a period of time. Let's use 20 days as an example. You take the closing price for each of the previous 20 days, add these price numbers together, and then divide by 20. This gives you the average price for those 20 days. The next day you repeat the same process with the new set of numbers:

the oldest day from your previous calculation gets dropped out because it is no longer in your 20-day range and the most recent closing price replaces it. As each day passes, you calculate a new 20-day SMA number that you can plot on a graph against the time. For the 50-day and the 200-day SMAs, you go through the same process with the corresponding number of days.

If the stock price you are plotting is constantly moving down, then the moving average prices get dragged lower as well. This gives you a trendline that you can monitor for trend changes. In our example, if the price reverses and starts to move higher, then the stock price will eventually cross the moving average, which has been lagging behind the current price movement. This cross provides a possible indicator of a change in sentiment.

Figure 8.5 shows a plot of Micron Technology, Inc. (MU) trending lower with the moving averages following the price down until it starts to reverse. On August 14th, MU's price crosses over the 20-day SMA. This is a sign of a possible change in investor sentiment with a new uptrend beginning. In our MU example, the price consolidates (churns sideways) for almost 2 weeks until the price starts to break above the 50-day SMA. After this event, the price trend change is clearly established and MU's stock price moves higher.

The chart of MU also shows how for a number of times the 20-day SMA acts as a support as the stock moves higher with waves of buying and selling. This illustrates how moving averages can be used to get a good entry in a trade and also to keep you in the trade in order to maximize profits.

The exponential moving average calculation is a little more complicated so I will not provide an explanation of it in this book. The formulas used are readily available on the Internet. The important thing to know when comparing the 2 different moving averages is that the EMA is more sensitive to recent changes in the price of the stock. This means that the EMA will react more quickly and, depending upon the situation, may or may not be good.

Because the EMA reacts faster when the price changes direction, it can provide an earlier signal of a possible change in trend. But, especially during times of higher volatility, this quicker reaction can also give the wrong signal. Stocks move in waves regardless of what direction they are moving: up, down or sideways. If a stock in a downtrend starts to bounce higher after a wave of selling, the EMA could start pointing up and potentially send a signal that there is an overall change in direction of the stock's price. This may not be the case if it is just a temporary bounce higher before continuing on a downtrend. Therefore this early indicator can result in a false trend change signal.

Because the SMA moves more slowly, it can keep you in a winning trade longer by smoothing out the inevitable bounces or pullbacks that normally occur during a long-term trend. Conversely, this slower moving trend line may also keep you in a trade when the trend has actually changed, so you may have to use other tools or fundamental analysis to decide if this trend is changing to the other direction. You will more often use the SMA when you are in your trades for longer durations and you are thus wanting to stay with a trend for as long as possible.

Due to the different levels of sensitivity between the 2 types of moving averages, you should consider adjusting which one to use based on the particular market environment. In volatile markets, where prices are bouncing up and down, an SMA may be a better tool. In less volatile market conditions, you would consider using the EMA to get earlier entry signals on trend changes.

Referring to Figure 8.6, you can see the difference between using the 20-day SMA versus the 20-day EMA. You'll notice that the EMA gives a slightly earlier signal as the MU price first crosses the faster reacting moving average. In this case, you may have got a slightly lower entry price on the trade, however, given the great run on MU it would not have made a big difference in your total return on the trade.

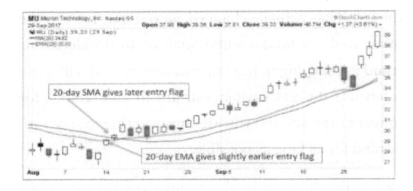

Moving Average Time Periods

As a swing trader using moving averages tools, you will need to consider what periods of time you want to use that give the best signals for your trading style. The first thing you should do is to stay with some of the periods that are commonly used by traders and computers. As I have discussed already, these moving averages work as technical indicators because they are, in effect, self-fulfilling prophecies. Many other traders and machines are looking at the same indicators and they work in part because of that fact.

The shorter the number of days used to calculate the moving average, the sooner you will see a change in direction because the short time periods more strongly reflect current price action. Like the EMA, these shorter time frames can be good in identifying a shift

104

in sentiment between the buyers and sellers, but they can also give false signals by reflecting the waves of buying and selling that occur within the typical wave action movements of a stock's price.

The most common periods used by swing traders are 20-day, 50-day and 200-day SMAs. Because traders are watching price movements in relation to these averages, they usually offer areas of support and resistance. The 200-day SMA is highly revered and normally provides the strongest level of support when a stock is selling off and the strongest level of resistance when a stock is starting to move higher from a low.

Traders also use the percentage of stocks in the market that are trading above their 200-day average as a gauge to determine the overall health of the stock market. The higher the percentage of stocks above their 200-day SMA, the more the overall market is biased to trending higher, therefore, the better trades for a swing trader may be long trades versus going short.

Below are some further thoughts to consider in developing your strategies related to using moving averages when swing trading:

The 20-day SMA is a good tool to use for a short-term swing trade. In a trending stock, the price action will often respect this level and it will also quickly identify a shift in sentiment and thus a reversal in trend.

The 20-day EMA is a faster reacting tool that can be used for short-term swing trades. It can get you into a trade earlier but in more volatile markets, it can also give you a false trend reversal signal.

The 50-day SMA is also a popular gauge for a longer-term swing trade and it will allow you to ride a potentially profitable trade longer in order to make additional gains. It is a good intermediate balance between the shorter 20-day and the longer 200-day SMAs.

The 200-day SMA represents almost 1 year of past price action (there are about 250 trading days in a year). In a down trending stock, this SMA may provide significant support and therefore be a good entry for a long position due to it being a very popular level for traders (remember the discussion on self-fulfilling prophecies). The risk on this sort of trade is when the price finds a support level just below the 200-day SMA and the trader is then stopped out.

The Golden Cross and the Death Cross

One other way to use moving averages to determine a directional price change is to watch for what traders refer to as a "golden cross" or a "death cross". This indicator uses the 50-day and 200-day SMAs. For example, let's consider a stock that has been in a long-term downtrend. Due to this trend, the 50-day moving average is creating a line that is below the 200-day SMA line. A golden cross signal on this stock will occur when the 50-day SMA crosses the 200-day moving average from below to above. When this happens, it is an indication that the negative sentiment is possibly changing with the downtrend in price shifting to an uptrend. This cross happens because the 50-day SMA is reflecting more current price action while the 200-day SMA is lagging further behind, reflecting prices that are further in the past.

The death cross is the opposite of the golden cross. It occurs when a stock is in a general uptrend and the price action starts to trend lower. Once again, the faster-reacting 50-day SMA starts to turn down faster than the slower reacting 200-day SMA and they eventually cross. The 50-day SMA crosses from above the 200-day SMA to below it, showing a change in sentiment and stock price direction.

Moving Averages in Range-Bound Stocks and Markets

As a swing trader, you need to be aware that SMA and EMA tools do not work well in markets or in stocks that are trading in a limited range (where the price makes relatively small moves between support and resistance). This type of market or stock is referred to as being "range-bound", and the price action is commonly referred to as "churning". In these range-bound trading cases, all of the different time period SMA and EMA lines ripple sideways between levels of support and resistance. The price action does not

108

respect these lines, therefore, these tools are most effective when trends are occurring: either higher or lower.

How to Use Moving Averages

You can also monitor these averages once you have entered a trade in order to help you to decide whether to exit a trade completely at a target price or to take some of the position off at one target and continue to hold the rest as the stock price continues to move in your favor. This is referred to as "scaling out" and will be discussed later in the book.

The SMA can be used to find a potential area of support or resistance. For example, if you are holding a short position, you might consider covering all or some of that short position as the price of the stock approaches the 200-day SMA, which is watched by many traders and trading machines as an area of significant support.

Moving averages can be used as an indicator to enter a trade, to exit a trade and to stay in an existing trade. Therefore, it is a good tool in your arsenal when markets and/or stocks are trending up or down.

Relative Strength Index

The Relative Strength Index (RSI) is another indicator that you can use to help you pick a good entry or exit on a stock. The index was developed by J. Welles Wilder and is an indicator that measures the speed and change of price movements. Some traders refer to it as a "momentum oscillator".

Many professional technicians believe that stocks are constantly moving between a position of being overvalued or undervalued and that their true value lies in the middle of these wave actions. Occasionally, stocks will become extremely overvalued or undervalued. The RSI is one way to measure how much over or undervalued a stock might be.

The RSI calculation generates a number that ranges between zero and 100. I will not discuss or show the formula that is used to calculate this number but, for those interested, it is readily available on the Internet. Almost every trading platform will do this calculation for you. As a swing trader, you only really need to understand what the RSI number is telling you about a stock's price action.

The RSI will never actually reach zero or 100 but traders who use the RSI get interested in stocks that are either below 30 or above 70 on the index. A number above 70 will indicate that a stock's price has been rising strongly to the point it may be getting overbought or extended to the upside in price. Conversely, a RSI number that is below 30 indicates that a stock's price has been in a strong downward move and might be getting oversold or extended to the downside. Index readings above or below these numbers provide an indication that the stock price may be due for a reversal in price trend. In the case of a stock selling off with an RSI of 23 for example, it might mean the stock could reverse and the price will start to move higher, even if only temporarily.

While some traders use 30 and 70 as levels to watch, I prefer 20 and 80 for swing trading because these are more extreme levels of overbought and oversold and therefore give a more definitive signal on potential topping and bottoming price action. The downside of using these more extreme levels of 20 and 80 is that some changes in sentiment could be missed and a reversal will happen before the RSI reaches these levels.

In an uptrending market, the RSI value will run between 45 and 85, with the 45 area on the index acting as support. A downtrending market will result in RSI values of 15 to 55, with resistance being around 55.

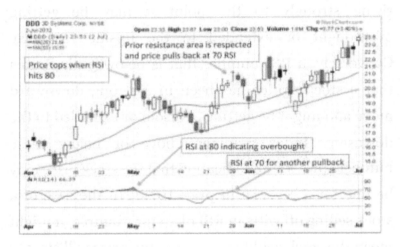

Figure 8.8 is a chart of 3D Systems Corporation (DDD) and shows how the extreme level of the RSI (over 80) predicted a subsequent drop in the price of DDD. On the next wave of buying in DDD, the RSI only reached the 70 level before another drop in price occurred.

How to Use the RSI Indicator

The RSI is a good indicator for you to employ and can be used to scan for potential trades on its own or in combination with other indicators. It can be used to indicate when stocks have been either overbought or oversold. When a stock is getting overbought and the RSI reaches 80 or higher, the price has risen to an extreme level and may be due for a price drop. When the RSI drops to 20 or below, then the price action on a stock is getting much oversold and may be due for a reversal and a subsequent bounce higher.

These trend reversals can be temporary and the stock may return to the original trend or it could indicate some bottoming or topping action in the stock price. I do not suggest that the RSI is a good stand-alone indicator as it is better used in combination with the other tools and indicators discussed in this book to confirm if a bottoming or topping in price action is happening.

MACD: Convergence and Divergence

As I discussed in the previous sections, spotting a reversal offers an opportunity to take advantage of a profitable trade in a stock. Spotting a trend change consistently and getting a good entry on that change is equivalent to finding the Holy Grail of swing trading. Another common reversal tracking tool used by traders is the Moving Average Convergence Divergence, which is commonly referred to as the MACD. This tool measures the momentum of a stock and is intended to help you spot a change in the sentiment of the market or in a stock.

Although the momentum of a stock will trend just like the price, changes in momentum will often precede changes in price. Imagine you get in your car, put it in drive and push down on the accelerator - you begin to move forward and pick up speed. If you keep your foot on the gas pedal, you will keep going faster until the resistance outside of the car builds up to a point where you are in equilibrium between the resistance of the wind and the force applied by the engine. If you now take your foot off of the gas, you will start to gradually slow down. The car is still moving forward but it is decelerating in speed.

Now think of your car's movement in terms of the price of a stock. Your foot is off of the gas, and the car is still moving forward (the stock price is still going up), however, both the car and the stock price are slowing down. Eventually, the car stops (the price stops moving up) and if it is on a hill, it starts rolling backward (the price starts dropping). The MACD calculation allows you to see this gradual change in sentiment between the buyers and the sellers before the price reflects this change happening.

The MACD was developed by Gerald Appel to chart the momentum of a stock by measuring the increasing and decreasing space between short-term and long-term exponential moving averages. Traders use different time frames to calculate their 2 moving averages depending on their preferences but typical periods are the 12-day and the 26-day. The shorter period moving average (12-day) is always closer to the current price when a stock is consistently moving one way or another. The longer period moving average lags a trending stock's current price. Therefore, as the price starts to level off, these 2 moving averages start to converge or come together. The price of the stock may continue to rise or fall but the rate may be slowing which causes the convergence or coming together of the 2 moving averages.

If the stock price is accelerating higher, the 2 averages will move apart or diverge with the short-term moving average moving more aggressively higher compared to the longer-term average.

A visual representation of the MACD is a graph that shows the distance between the 2 moving averages as seen in Figure 8.9, a chart of the Consumer Staples Select Sector SPDR Fund (XLP). There are 2 lines that represent the 2 different SMAs and a bar chart that represents the distance between the 2 moving averages. The bars that are increasing in size mean that the moving averages are moving further apart and thus representing a continuation in the price trend (either higher or lower). When the bars start to decrease in size, the distance between the 2 moving averages is decreasing and a possible reversal in trend may be coming.

In Figure 8.9, the chart of XLP shows how the MACD tracks the price move higher while the RSI starts to signal that the stock is overbought. If a long trader was just looking at the RSI alone, they would have missed a big price move up, as the MACD continued to show good price strength. As the price movement started to top around June 5th, the MACD bars became shorter, indicating the moving averages were converging and the uptrend price action was running out of momentum and that it was a good time to exit if you were long.

Since both the RSI and the MACD are momentum indicators, you might ask, what is the difference between the 2 measures? The main difference lies in what each is designed to measure. The MACD is primarily used to gauge the strength of price movement while the RSI provides an indication as to whether the market or a particular stock is in an overbought or oversold condition in relation to recent high or low prices.

You should be aware that the 2 indicators are measuring different factors and, therefore, they sometimes give opposite or contrary indications. The RSI may be over 70 for a sustained period of time, indicating an overbought condition in relation to recent prices, while the MACD may indicate that the buying momentum in the same stock or market is still increasing.

Regardless, either indicator may assist you by signaling an upcoming trend change. When both indicators are aligned, it can provide you with a good indication of a continuing trend or reversal.

How to Use the MACD

Although the RSI is more commonly used as a momentum indicator, the MACD is another indicator that you can use to check the momentum of a stock's price action. When looking at charts of potential trade setups, the MACD and RSI charts can be overlaid to see if there is an alignment between these 2 momentum indicators. If there is, this will give you more confidence in taking a position.

It should be noted that some scanning tools include the RSI but do not include the MACD. Both are good indicators to support a swing trader's conviction for entering a trade. There are a number of different specific MACD strategies that some traders use for determining entries and exits that are beyond the scope of this book. As you develop your swing trading business, you may want to do a more in-depth study on MACD trading strategies, however, the tools that I discuss in this book should provide ample opportunities to find and make profitable trades.

Average True Range

The Average True Range (ATR) indicator was also developed by J. Welles Wilder. Initially aimed for use in trading commodities, it has since become more widely accepted as an indicator for other financial instruments such as stocks.

The ATR is an indicator that measures the "volatility" of price action or, in other words, how much a stock price can swing over a certain period of time (such as a day). Wilder designed the ATR with commodities and daily prices in mind because commodity price action can be more volatile than stock prices. Commodities will often gap up and gap down between trading sessions, therefore, a volatility formula based only on the high-low range during a trading session (ignoring the gaps) would fail to capture all of that volatility. The ATR indicator takes into account those gaps as well as the swings in price throughout a normal trading session.

I will not provide the details on the formulas used to calculate this indicator but they are readily available on the Internet for those wanting more details. Wilder started with a concept called true range, which takes into account the previous day's close to capture any gaps that might have occurred between trading sessions. Absolute values are used because he was interested in measuring the distance between 2 points and not the direction. Absolute values are all positive numbers, so in the case of a drop in price which is negative, the number becomes a positive (for example, -$0.75 becomes a +$0.75).

Figure 8.10 shows the price movement of Micron Technology, Inc. (MU) with a corresponding graph below showing the ATR value for each day. The ATR indicator will change over time as shown in the chart and is dependent on the level of volatility that the stock is currently experiencing. As the daily price variation increases, so does the ATR.

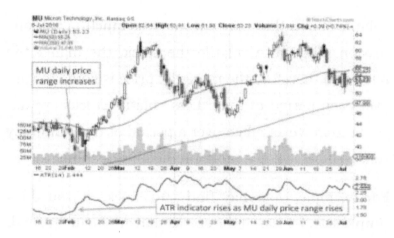

Because the ATR represents a range in the price of the stock, lower-priced stocks will have lower ATR values than higher-priced stocks. For example, a $25.00 stock will likely have a much lower ATR value than a $250.00 stock. This is because a 1% move in the higher-priced $250.00 stock will be much larger than a 1% move in the lower-priced $25.00 stock, which means that the ATR values are not comparable unless they are converted to percentages of the stock's price.

How to Use the ATR Indicator

If you are willing to take on more risk as a swing trader, the ATR indicator can be used to find stocks with extremely high volatility. In addition, the ATR indicator can be used to illuminate high volatility stocks in your scan in order to assist you in finding less volatile stocks that may not move as much in any one session. The more volatile the stock, the higher the ATR, and therefore the more the price is going to vary over each period of time. Less volatile stocks are not going to move as much over a period of time and may very well behave in a more predictable fashion.

For example, you may find 500 stocks if you do a simple scan to search the stocks that are in an uptrend. In a second scan, you may decide to eliminate the higher volatility stocks from the results, which may further reduce down to 100 the stock opportunities presented by the scan.

The ATR indicator can also tell you how much variation in price you can expect to see from day to day. Understanding daily volatility and movement on any one day will help keep you from being stopped out on a position because of the normal price variation that you would expect to experience given the ATR value for a particular stock. For example, let's imagine a stock with an ATR of $1.50. If you use a stop-loss of $0.50 from the current price, then it is more likely you will get stopped out due to the normal volatility of the stock.

There are other more advanced strategies for using the ATR as a trade decision tool. Some traders will use it as an exit indicator for an existing position. If a stock price closes more than one ATR value away from its most recent close, it is possible that a significant change in the sentiment of the stock has occurred.

Other traders have used the ATR as a trailing stop for a stock. Using a long position example, they will take the highest high since taking the position and subtract 2 times the ATR to determine a trailing stop price for their position. The use of the 2 times multiplier is somewhat subjective. Others will use 3 times the ATR to determine their stop out price level.

As a new swing trader, you will likely want to be aware of this indicator only as a measure of volatility. Once you gain more comfort and experience with the various indicators, you can look at expanding your use of the ATR.

Horizontal support and resistance lines are one of the most common tools and are relatively easy for novice swing traders to learn how to use.

When a swing trader refers to a stock's chart, it should be apparent that, in the past, there were areas of support where its price traded down to a certain level, and then it either paused or reversed to go higher. This would be a level of support.

There should also be areas that can be identified where a stock moved higher to a point and then the price movement either stalled and consolidated or dropped back. This is an area of resistance.

By connecting the areas of support and resistance with horizontal lines, a swing trader can identify these price levels which will likely be in play with future price moves. A break above a prior level of resistance or a break below a prior level of support indicates a trend continuation and possible entry for a trader.

Diagonal lines can also be drawn in a stock that is either trending up or down to create a channel of trading in that trend. A break of the channel may indicate a change in sentiment.

Moving averages are another tool that is commonly used by swing traders and computers. The 2 common moving averages are the simple moving average (SMA) and the exponential moving average (EMA). The EMA responds faster to potential changes in price direction, which can get a trader into a trade sooner. The upside is a potentially more profitable trade but the downside is that it could be providing an indication of a false trend change. A false trend change indication often happens when the market is more volatile with more price swings.

There are a number of different time periods that the moving averages are commonly calculated for. These include the 20-day, 50-day and 200-day periods. The shorter periods respond faster to price changes and shifts in sentiment.

The Relative Strength Index (RSI) is a momentum oscillator that can be used to determine if the price of a stock is at an extreme level compared to its recent price. Stocks move between levels of being overbought or oversold and on occasion these situations become extreme. Whenever the RSI is below 20 (oversold) or over 80 (overbought), a possible reversal trade opportunity is being represented.

The Moving Average Convergence Divergence (MACD) measures the momentum of a stock's price movement and can be an indicator of a trend reversal using 2 EMAs. A shorter period EMA is compared to a longer period EMA and the distance measured between the 2 can be used to flag either a price trend reversal or continued strength in a trend.

The Average True Range (ATR) is an indicator that measures the "volatility" of price action. It measures how much a stock price can swing over a certain period of time such as a day and incorporates the gap up and gap down action that can occur between individual trading days. The ATR is a good number to know so that stops are not set so close to the current price that they will get triggered on an average day of price swings.

Made in the USA
Monee, IL
25 November 2021

Made in the USA
Las Vegas, NV
25 November 2024

12591275R00075